GETTING SMARTER

GETTING SMARTER
by
Julia First

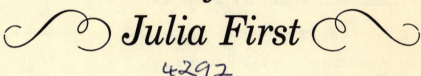

Prentice-Hall, Inc.,
Englewood Cliffs, New Jersey

10 9 8 7 6 5 4 3 2 1

Printed in the United States of America • J

Prentice-Hall International, Inc., London
Prentice-Hall of Australia, Pty. Ltd., North Sydney
Prentice-Hall of Canada, Ltd., Toronto
Prentice-Hall of India Private Ltd., New Delhi
Prentice-Hall of Japan, Inc., Tokyo

Book Design by Dann Jacobus

Library of Congress Cataloging in Publication Data

Library of Congress Cataloging in Publication
Data

First, Julia.
    Getting smarter.

    SUMMARY: A mother's venture into the
working world results in a new sense of freedom
for her but new restrictions for her twelve-year-
old daughter.
    [1. Mothers and daughters—Fiction.
2. Mothers—Employment—Fiction] I. Title.
PZ7.F49875Ge   [Fic]   74-5104
ISBN 0-13-354829-5

For My Husband

Chapter 1

It was so dark I could hardly see my hand in front of my face. Actually, my hand wasn't in front of my face. It was clenched in my lap as I peered at the eye chart in Dr. Clement's office. My mother took me there because the dumb cluck school nurse decided I had faulty vision. As though being flat chested and buck-toothed wasn't enough, without glasses! One more physical impediment and I would definitely not be able to cope.

"Mom," I had said to her on the way to Dr. Clement's, "I do *not* need glasses. I can see fine. All I need is good light and big print and I'm in."

But I didn't really believe a word I said. I'd suspected for a couple of months that something was wrong, when I had to hold my books about an inch away from my face to decode the print.

"We'll see what the doctor says."

Sitting in the waiting room I had counted six patients: one with an eye patch, two with tinted motorcycle goggles, two with regular sunglasses and one without any glasses, whose eyes were red and runny. But worst of all I was the only kid there. They were all middle-aged types, which didn't do a thing for my morale. It sure proved I was in a definite minority of one in my age and sex group with the horrible eye condition I had.

When my turn came, I think my morale sank lower because my mother accompanied me. Actually, I wasn't sure how I felt about that. On the one hand, it made me look like a baby; on the other, it was bound to be pretty scary in there.

Dr. Clement began by asking me about thirty stupid questions starting with did I ever have dizzy spells? Did I ever faint? Did I ever see double? When I said no to all three, I figured I might get off easy—maybe he'd just say, forget it. But no, after he finished giving me the third degree, he had me sit in a contraption that was worse than the dentist's chair. Then he darkened the room and put me through a twenty-minute ordeal.

It wasn't anything painful, just weird. On the wall at the other end of the room there was a big circle with a pencil line going up and down and another going across the middle. He turned a red light on the circle, and I was supposed to tell him if it was left or right, or above or below the lines. Then he flashed a light in my eyes, real close, so you'd expect it to come out the back of your head. Reading the letters of the alphabet was the last thing I had to do.

When I couldn't tell an A from an N on the chart, he

2

switched on the lights. I was afraid to look at his face. Instead, I concentrated on the medical equipment he had lined up. There was a giant X-ray machine and an eight-foot monster that looked as if it was going to jump on me any second and pin me on the floor.

"You need glasses, all right, Rona," Dr. Clement said calmly. *He* didn't have to wear them, so why should *he* get excited? But *me* in glasses!

Right away you can see the picture. From my outward appearance I could now pass for, say, an intellectual. Not that that's so bad, but I don't happen to be the type. The closest I come to this category is writing for our school newspaper, the Horace Mann *Horn*. Not articles, exactly. I write poems. I have a knack, nothing inspiring, really. But, for instance, when Miss Peters became Mrs. Holmes, I wrote her a welcome-back-to-Horace-Mann-School-poem:

We missed you when you left a miss.
We're glad you're back a Mrs.
We hope you stay a good long time,
Your class, with love and kisses.

Of course the boys weren't too crazy about the love and kisses part, but since it rhymed so well, they signed it.

After Dr. Clement signed the prescription, my mother dragged me to the optician. I kept whining, "Mom, don't make me wear glasses. I'm already a mess."

All my mother said was, "Rona, the doctor said you need glasses. What are you talking about?"

"How come you didn't deny I'm a mess?"

"There's nothing to deny." Then right away she contradicted her own statement trying to make me feel better. "You'll outgrow it." After which she delivered her ultimatum: "And you *have* to wear glasses."

"Mom," I piped up in my best whine, "why can't I get contact lenses?"

"Contact lenses! You're crazy! Do you realize what they cost?"

Chapter 2

The glasses were ready in a couple of days, and I picked them up on my way home from school.

"Enjoy them, Rona," Mr. Adams had the gall to say when he handed them to me. Gall was nothing compared to his attitude of thinly disguised ridicule when I told him I wasn't going to put them on just yet. He's another one that doesn't need to wear glasses. For all I know he has contacts.

When I got in the house, I modeled them for my mother. "Now aren't you ashamed having a daughter that looks like me?" I asked hoping that would persuade her to buy me contacts.

My mother happens to be very pretty, and I think it must have been a terrible blow to her when she found out that her only daughter looked like her husband. I love my father, and he certainly isn't ugly, but for a girl to look like him isn't really something a mother can take lightly no matter what she says.

"What my daughter looks like does not make me ashamed, but the value my daughter puts on her appearance is something that does."

Why is it, I wonder, every time someone tells you not to worry about something, it happens that that particular something is one worry they don't have.

"Mom," I said, "you've got a terrific way of not coming right out and saying what you really mean."

"What I mean is, glasses do not make a person beautiful or homely."

"Yeah but, tough for me, not everyone sees it your way."

"People who count in your life see it that way."

I groaned and whined at the same time, "Paul Wallace counts a whole bunch in my life, and he won't take any of my poems now. It will be too much for him to have to look at me for the second it takes to hand him a piece of paper."

Paul is the editor–in–chief of the *Horn*. He's in the eighth, two grades ahead of me. He also happens to be the best-looking boy in the whole school. In the world, probably. He has this dark curly hair and a nose I myself would be proud to own. And his teeth! Straight and white. And those green eyes!

"Rona, you may not know this, but I am very tired of hearing about Paul Wallace."

My father wasn't too hot about making me feel I was divine either. It wasn't so much what he said, but it took him a full six seconds of looking before he was able to say *anything*. And his first words didn't sound as if he had much confidence in them. "That's a real attractive shade of pink. Looks very well on you, Rona."

I guess he wanted to say something nice. I didn't bother to tell him that the color wasn't my taste.

Dinner that night was an experience. First of all, there was the usual seating arrangement, and with my glasses on, it was even less bearable than before. My two brothers, Doug and Kenny, ages eight and six respectively, sat opposite me and now I could see them better. Even though they irritate the life out of me, I have to admit they're both good-looking kids, Kenny in particular. He looks like my mother. Right away you can see how that hurts and how unfair it is. I figure if they had only one bad eye apiece, they could use my pair of glasses between them and they'd still be better looking than I am even without glasses.

So there we were drinking soup, with my brothers making the most disgusting noises getting it down. In between slurps they'd stop and stare at me.

"Can you really see out of those things?" Kenny asked me.

Before I could answer, his brother chimed in, "Is that glass or wood?"

I made up my mind I was going to push their faces in as soon as I got them alone.

Then, out of a clear blue sky, my mother came out with, "Arnie, do you realize the price of contact lenses—two hundred dollars."

I turned as pink as my frames, my insides did somersaults, and my fingers became icicles. She's going to get me contacts!

7

My father, just glared back at my mother. "Contact lenses! Who needs contact lenses? You out of your mind?" He started looking wildly around the table.

"Arnie, it's not who needs, it's how much it costs. Things are high. Everything is high." She gave him a real flat-across-the-table look.

Then I knew what she was working up to. Herself and a job. She was going to put it on a we-need-money-to-pay-for-the-everyday-expenses basis. Not contacts, that was for sure. My fingers stayed cold, but my color went back to pale and my insides settled back to their normal position.

"Costs!" he practically shouted. "Don't I know what things cost today? Corn beef, tongue, roast beef—even cabbage to make cole slaw is sky-high. Cabbage today costs what corn beef did yesterday. Pass the mustard, Rona."

I passed.

Daddy sploshed it on his pot roast. If there's anything my father is crazy about it's pot roast and mustard. In fact, my mother makes the *mustard* too. For my part I can do without mustard for the rest of my life, but if my father's eyes don't water and if he doesn't cough after one forkful, it's not strong enough.

My mother looked pleased. I didn't think it was because Daddy approved of her mustard, but because now she could get on with more job talk.

"I got a call from Charlotte today," she said.

"So?" Daddy said.

Charlotte is Mrs. Daniels, one of my mother's friends, not my father's. He doesn't like her. He thinks she pushes my mother around.

"She . . . uh . . . she's very busy at her tour office."

Mrs. Daniels works for a guided-walking-tour service, and I've heard her begging my mother to go for an interview so she could be a tour guide. Of course I never knew till now that my mother took the idea seriously. It's a pretty exciting job, I guess. You get into the mayor's and the governor's offices, and you probably feel like a celebrity.

"So, good for her she's busy at the tour office." I could see my father couldn't care less. "Kenny, stop wolfing your food."

My mother was barely nibbling her salad. "Well, she says they could use me and they'd like me to . . . to stop in tomorrow and . . . check it out."

My father put his fork down on his plate, hard. He looked up slowly not moving his head or blinking his eyes, with a burning look as if the mustard was going to seep out.

"Ooh Mom, you gonna be a tour guide? Can I come?" Doug asked.

"If he can go, so can I," his echo said.

My parents ignored them both.

"Take it easy," my mother said to Daddy.

"How can I take it easy when my wife gets an itch that she has to strike out for herself?"

"Arnie, it's about time that I get liberated like other women and have a career of my own."

"What is this with a career? You have a perfectly good career with life tenure in the store."

"Arnie," she answered him with a new, independent tone in her voice, "there is absolutely no redeeming personal value in my being a sandwich girl to a bunch of dirty, unkempt college kids."

Our deli is on the same block as a dormitory of one of

9

the city colleges around the corner from us. I guess for my father to lose his best waitress and general aide was as bad for him as wearing glasses was for me. He was practically in tears.

"Those dirty, unkempt kids are our bread and butter, Dorothy."

"My working on the outside will supplement our bread and butter. Before you know it, Arnie, we will be paying something like four thousand dollars a year per child for college tuition." She was pretty wound up.

"At the rate Charlotte will pay you, our children will have children of their own before you can earn their tuition."

"Then there is no better time to start than the present."

My father kept on with his rebuttal. "Who will replace you in the store?"

"Advertise."

"Good help is impossible to get—you know that. And even if I'm lucky, it may take months."

"Rona can help out until you can get someone else. She's big enough now, aren't you, dear?"

Rona! I almost choked on that.

Daddy came to my rescue. "Rona isn't big enough or old enough. She's only eleven."

I just lost six months of my life.

Mom said, "For all practical purposes, she's twelve."

"Dorothy, you know children aren't allowed to work until they're fourteen."

"It will only be temporary, Arnie. And she won't be on the payroll."

Oh, that made it even better.

"You can't be replaced, Dorothy. The kids love you."

"They'll learn to love Rona."

What *I* loved was the way they were talking right in front of me as if I weren't there. "Do I get to say something about this?" I asked.

"Rona, will you take the job for a cash gift?" my mother wanted to know.

"No," I said.

My parents looked at each other and then my mother said, "A very special bonus at the end of the week?"

My father shook his head as if to say business would fall off and he'd go into bankruptcy.

I started to say no again when my glasses slipped down my nose. I began to realize that I had to get money from somewhere. I couldn't go around looking like a zombi forever. And the most awful thing about my face wer these glasses. These awful pink panes that slid down m nose, and distorted my otherwise undistinguished orb But after I agreed, I realized my mistake. It meant givi up two hours every afternoon. So I never got to see Pa Wallace. At least he wouldn't have to look at me in current state of repulsiveness.

My father didn't even notice that I was sacrificing life. He was still trying to talk Mom out of the d "Who'll take care of the boys, Dorothy? During worl hours it is impractical for me to assume the responsibili

Doug and Kenny were no bargain for anyone to care of. What *would* my mother do with them? She for work in the store after my brothers came home school, and then they'd report in to her every little v

When Daddy said, "the boys," Kenny burst into

"You're gonna send me away!"

What a great idea, I thought.

My mother squeezed his hand across the table. "Sweetheart, baby, don't you *ever* think such a thing! We're not sending *anyone* away, darling."

He stopped crying and I nearly threw up. My father was breathing hard, waiting for my mother to come up with a solution.

"Arnie, I want you to know I have considered this very carefully." My mother was setting him straight on *her* responsibility. "I called Mrs. Porter to see if she could keep an extra eye out for them."

"I like Mrs. Porter!" Doug was enthusiastic. "She gives us lots of candy."

Mrs. Porter was the mother of their friends, Joey and Ralph. Where she was going to get that "extra eye," I couldn't imagine.

"Mrs. Porter is not adequate," my father said.

"I realized that Arnie, so I called the Y. Mr. Brody has an afternoon program that should work out very well. The boys will go to the store directly from school, and the station wagon will pick them up there."

Kenny got excited. "You mean we can go swimming?"

"And play basketball!" Doug's eyes were popping. Doug is tall for his age and he seriously thinks he's going to be asked to play pro basketball by the time he's in high school.

"You see, Arnie." My mother wagged her head at him. "It's a good program."

"It also takes money," he reminded her.

"They can't be adequately taken care of for nothing, Arnie. You can't have it both ways."

"I just want it the way it's always been," my father answered.

"The way it's always been, Arnie, no longer is. Times change."

"Dorothy, you're making a big mistake," my father warned her.

I silently seconded the thought.

After that, outside of Doug and Kenny, nobody had much appetite and dinner wasn't even over. I took some plates off the table. My mother came in the kitchen and started dishing out the dessert.

"There's really no reason for Daddy to get excited. I might not get the job," she told me nervously.

I couldn't say anything. Nobody remembered me and my plight. Glasses *and* working in the stupid store. What a ghastly combination. No matter what bothered my mother and father, nobody felt worse than I. The only optimistic thing I could think of was that maybe she won't get the job.

Chapter 3

The way Mom acted before her interview, you'd think she was applying for the position of first woman president of the United States.

"How do I look, Rona? My slip showing? My lipstick on straight?"

I was the last person she should have asked for encouragement, since I certainly hoped she wouldn't get hired. As a matter of fact, I had a strange feeling that she hoped so too. But she got the job.

Mom was starting her new job the same day I was going to show up in the school wearing my glasses for the first time. That Tuesday was bad news from the minute I woke up. Or rather got woked up by the noise from the kitchen.

"Doug, don't forget, wait for Kenny after school, the

same as always, and go right to the deli to check in with Daddy. Mr. Brody will pick you up in his station wagon."

"What about a snack, Mom?" Doug was asking with a mouthful of crackle-and-pop cereal. I could tell even from two rooms away what he had in his full mouth. He always eats the same cereal for breakfast, and he always talks while he eats no matter how many times he's told not to.

"Doug, don't talk with food in your mouth," I heard my mother tell him. "I'm making a snack for you and Kenny now. Daddy will take it to the store with him."

"Mom, are we going to have to do what Rona tells us?" That was Doug in between mouthfuls. Frankly I wasn't interested in telling either of those kids to do anything except buzz off. All I wanted to do was get a new pair of eyes that didn't need glasses and I'd probably settle for any color.

"You will do what your father tells you. Rona will be busy working in the store."

I could hardly wait.

"Arnie," she called to my father, "hurry out of the bathroom. I have to take a shower, and Charlotte told me to be there at eight."

My father opened the bathroom door a couple of cracks and put his lathered face up close. He also raised his voice. "What do you mean, Charlotte told you? Since when are you taking orders from Charlotte Daniels?"

"Oh, Arnie, you know what l mean. After all, I am working for her."

"I don't recall you took orders from me when—"

"Arnie, dear, please! I'm in a hurry. This is my first day. Have a heart."

When my mother says "please" at the end of a sentence, everybody's supposed to know she's had it. Usually, but not always, we give in to her at that point. I guess my father understood that when a person is starting something new she could be nervous, because he didn't say anything more.

"I'll be home at five thirty, and I've made supper. Rona!" That was my signal. I went in the kitchen. She had the refrigerator door open, showing me all the pots, and told me what I was supposed to do with them at five o'clock. I was thrilled. What I love to do after a happy day at school is to work in a delicatessen and then come home and put pots in the oven.

"Got it, Rona?"

"Sure, Mom. I've got it." Got the hives is what I've got, I thought. Oh well, the new regime will probably take my mind off my eye problem at least.

"You look dumb, Rona." That was my darling brother Doug doing his bit to take my mind off my eye problem.

"Does it hurt your nose, Rona?" My brother Kenny.

"Shut up," I told both of them.

"Rona, that's not necessary." My mother.

"Okay, okay."

Yesterday, I thought to myself as I stepped out of our apartment building onto the sidewalk, I walked down these streets without glasses. What bad could happen if I didn't wear them today—on the way to school at least? I took them off and was surprised to notice quite a difference, like not being too sure about distances between sidewalk curbs and gutters. But I didn't have the strength of character to walk to school cold with them. My classmates and I would have

to get used to the new face gradually. And Paul Wallace—
well, I hated to think of his reaction.

I got to the next corner, Buswell Street, where Sharon
Simmons and I always meet. Sharon is my best friend. She
is a very unusual girl. She is well on the way to having what
I and every girl in the world wants—a 38C shape. The particular thing that makes Sharon unusual is that she couldn't
care less. She acts as if the size was more of a handicap
than an asset. For instance, she'll say, "It's bad enough
now, but if I keep growing in this direction I'll never make
it as a ballet dancer."

According to her, ballet dancers are supposed to have
flat bosoms, the reason being that nothing should divert
attention from the feet. Ballet is Sharon's passion. Every
Saturday morning she goes to Madame LaPierre for her
lesson. Her father says it costs a fortune, but her mother
says you shouldn't thwart a child's gift from God. Boy, I'll
say she's gifted. It's a lucky thing for me, though, that I'm
not interested in ballet, because with the tight price-control
program in my family I'd never get to take lessons.

It was no trouble at all for me to make Sharon out
without my glasses.

"Hi, Shar."

"Hi, Rone." She looked in the direction of my drab,
gray eyes.

"Did you get them?"

"Yeah."

"Let's see."

You'll get sick to your stomach."

"C'mon, let's see. It can't be that bad."

I looked around and ducked into a doorway. I put on

17

my glasses and held my head in one position, so she could get the full treatment.

She just kept looking without saying a word.

"Well?"

"We-ell. It could be worse."

"How?"

"I've seen people with thicker panes."

"They're called lenses."

Sharon was thinking. I could tell by her eyes, which happen to be a gorgeous golden brown. Some people have more than their fair share, I thought.

Finally she came out with, "Don't feel bad."

"Why not?" I said, feeling terrible.

"Well, I mean, if you can see better, that's the most important thing, isn't it?"

"I wouldn't say so," I said. "The most important thing, Shar, is to be beautiful and have a dream shape and be real cool about the whole thing."

"Those are three things and I don't think any of them is the most important thing at all."

"Naturally you don't, because you have at least one of them—the second thing, to be perfectly precise."

"It's not as great as you think. Everybody stares at you."

"What's wrong with that?"

"Rone, is that all you want? To be a sex symbol?" She sounded disgusted with me.

Me, a sex symbol. Wow!

She went on, "It's definitely not the "in" thing anymore. The style now is the Gloria Steinem look, and she wears glasses. And besides that, you ought to have some ambition for personal achievement."

I realized of course that she was right. "Shar, there are other important things in the world. And I guess my first ambition is to be a great poet, but I'd still like to be beautiful, too." And if the thought of being a great poet weren't depressing enough, who should come around the corner but Carol Fowler, one of the girls in our class.

I really have nothing against a girl just because she happens to be pretty. But someone who is pretty and flaunts it is something else. Carol not only has hair that shines, but she keeps shaking her head so you'll notice it. She also has a perfectly good pair of eyes. And on top of that, she has one of those faces that looks good at any angle. She is proudest of her profile and poses a lot, side view, while you're talking to her.

"Rona, you're wearing glasses!" she blurted without even having the grace to say hello first.

For about two seconds I had forgotten. But nobody was going to let me, I could see that. I didn't have any prepared remarks, so I didn't answer her. Then all of a sudden I got gutsy and decided to leave them on.

The three of us started walking. Trudy Kane and Bev Baker caught up with us.

"Rona, you're wearing glasses!" That was from Trudy.

"How did you know?" Some prepared remark.

"It's obvious, that's how, and don't get mad," she said.

"Who's mad? I'm insane with happiness."

Bev studied me. "I'll concede you're no competition for Raquel Welch," she said, "but, well . . . ."

"Boy, with friends like you," I said.

By the time we got to school and in our room, everyone in my class had been revoltingly exposed to Rona Cooper, nearsighted girl ape in disguise. I listened very hard and nobody said, "Rona, what an improvement."

But I'll have to admit that it was easier locating the chalk board and finding my place in my books. In fact, I had a very successful morning in math due to my improved vision, which did nothing to improve my looks. Then Janet Currier's crack was the next-to-the-last straw. Janet is not on my close-friend list. And never will be.

"I heard that it's okay for kids to wear contacts, Rona. Wouldn't your parents let you have them?"

I suffered silently before I could answer, "No."

"Wouldn't you rather?"

That was the last straw. I curbed my urge to kick her and shrugged my shoulders. If I said anything I knew my voice would break.

I walked over to the bulletin board to get away from her and saw the notices, unblurred, for the first time.

Monday 1:30—2:30. Math Club.
That was yesterday and if I could I wouldn't.

Tuesday 2:00—3:00. Tryouts for Thanksgiving Assembly Program.
I might be interested but my employer won't give me time off.

Wednesday 2:00—3:00. Glee Club.
I certainly am interested but my employer still won't give me time off.

Thursday 2:00—3:00. Cooking Club.
Not on your life.

Friday 2:00—3:00. Horace Mann *Horn* Editorial Staff Meeting.

20

Now, that's for me. If it included contributing writers, which I was.

But I would also be a working girl on Friday from 2:00 to 4:00. My one chance would be that Daddy would get my replacement by then.

When the bell rang for lunch I thought I'd just as soon go hungry. It was one thing to have my own sixth-grade classmates see me with my new affliction, but to have the rest of the school observing would be too much.

I wasn't in the cafeteria two seconds before Doris Carter, who is no beauty herself, looked at me and gasped. She actually put her hand over her mouth as if she was witnessing a murder and didn't say a word. I gave her a dirty look but I don't know if that shows the same way as when your eyes are uncovered.

When I was in the food line, Mrs. Nash the cook, who has known me since first grade, said, "Rona, I hardly recognized you." I smiled. Well, not exactly. I showed my teeth. Maybe my buck-teeth would look more familiar to her.

I thought that would be the low point of the day until fate had Paul Wallace cross my path, carrying his lunch tray. I froze. I couldn't even turn away or pull off the hardware. He froze too, naturally. I mean, how could he help himself, having a shock like that? He recovered first.

"Hi, Rona." He moved a leg to let me know I was standin the way.

"Hi, Paul." I moved and let him pass.

Then and there I decided that I was going to get contacts one way or another if it was the last act of my natural life.

21

Chapter 4

After school Sharon walked me to the deli. "Did you ever know anyone who had a rottener fate, Shar? I will be scarred for life."

"I'm thinking about it, Rone."

"Shar, how can I get money fast so I can get the contacts? How?"

"What we really ought to think about is in case you don't raise the money at all." Sharon is such a practical-minded girl.

"What I'll do in that case," I said, "is commit suicide. I'll spend the first day on my new job working out the least painful way to go. Or," I continued, "I just might figure out the *most* painful. That way, my mother will feel the greatest remorse for not letting me have contacts. She will carry the heavy burden of my agonizing demise until . . . ."

"I'm not listening, Rone. What I'm thinking about is, look at it this way. You're eleven and a half, right? In a year and a half you'll be thirteen, right?"

"Brilliant, Shar. Brilliant."

"No, I mean it. You know, when a girl, or even anybody, gets to be thirteen, different things happen in the body—like chemical changes."

"Now is when I could use them. I don't think I can hold out till I'm thirteen."

"But you'll only have to wear the things for a year and a half. Then your eyes will change. You'll see like you never saw before. You will be a new person—a woman!" Sharon's face was glowing as if she had just created a new Mona Lisa or Venus de Milo.

"Only one thing wrong with that, Shar. You see, even if that were so, it's right now that I can't stand. It's every minute *now* when everyone is looking at me. I feel so uncomfortable, I wish I could disintegrate into nothing. Dust, just tiny little atoms of dust."

"Now you know how I feel when people stare at me," Sharon said. "Or worse, because when they notice me they try *not* to."

"Oh, Sharon, how can you compare that? At least you know that when people look at you, they like it. When they look at me, they get nauseous."

"Rone, staring is staring. What's the difference?" Her voice got a little high-pitched. Then we were both quiet. When we got to the deli I told her I'd call later.

"The minute you get home, Rone."

"Natch."

Sharon and I have been in the habit of seeing each other

every day from the time we meet on our way to school and Saturdays after her ballet lesson and once in a while on Sunday afternoons if we can get out of receiving or visiting relatives. In between those times we call each other up, because we always have plenty to talk about. So my working was going to be hard on both of us.

"Don't forget, the very minute," Sharon said again as I pushed open the glass door of the deli.

A new emotion grabbed me as soon as I got on the other side of the door. If my mother decided that for all practical purposes I was twelve, then for all present practical purposes this group of my father's customers were middle-aged adults. I wasn't exactly scared stiff . . . more like limp.

There must have been at least three million college people in there. It was just one big bunch of noise, and if you wanted to walk down an aisle to get to a table in the back, you couldn't because they were standing ninety in the aisles. Everyone in the place was talking, and it would have taken an air-raid alert to stop them. It was plain bedlam.

I squeezed myself past the counters, which are on the left, both take-out and eat-in. Cathy, the girl at the cash register on the right, looked stoned—from the noise, that is —and she was taking the money and time out to smile and say thank you just as if the place was a peaceful bird sanctuary.

I found myself taking deep, long breaths. Not because I needed air, but because of the outstanding thing about my father's delicatessen—the ecstatic aroma.

Daddy makes a lot of the food he sells, but in particular the pickles, the half-sours. He has these barrels and barrels of half-sours in the back room, so when people come in the store the smell drives them absolutely out of their minds. No matter what anybody orders, they always get a pickle thrown in. Daddy is so proud of his recipe he wants everyone to share the pleasure.

I pushed my way through the mob and saw my father looking very harried, as he waited on a customer. Not being gung-ho about any part of it and still feeling shaky about the whole deal, it was hard for me to look interested.

"Reporting for duty, Daddy." I edged my way in behind the counter.

He gave me a look that said as plain as day, I don't like your being here any more than you do. Out loud he said, "Your first duty is to go in the kitchen and wash your hands. Next, fill the pickle trays."

Boy, just like that. He must think I'm an old pro.

Then I guess he remembered because he added, like a daddy instead of the Boss, "Harry is out back. He'll show you."

Harry showed me. He gave me trays full of pickles and pointed in the direction of the counters. I made four trips carrying pickle trays, going back and forth from the kitchen to the counters. It was like a relay race.

Then the chorus of orders started.

"Rona, clear those back tables and make sure you don't leave any mustard or scraps of any kind."

"Rona, bring tray three over to table five. On the double, baby. We want fast turnover—this is our busiest time of the day."

I was surprised that my mother had stuck it out so long. I took a spare second to look at the big clock over the door. Two thirty. Those college kids apparently ate heavy meals any hour of the day. Let's see, if my weekly bonus came to, say, a dollar an hour, I would have to work two hundred hours to pay for the contacts. If it wasn't for the money . . . .

"Rona, give Sam a hand in the kitchen, will you?"

All this ordering around made me think of the two people in the world that really cared about me. Grandpa and Grandma Bennett. If ten grown-ups would be raving about how gorgeous my brothers were, I could always count on my grandparents to say, "Just look at our girl! Did you know that Rona writes for her school paper?" or anything else they'd think of on the spur of the moment about how great *I* was, too. But they had just retired to Arizona, and I lost my two best supporters. I could write to them, though, and hold my parents up for blackmail. I'd warn them that I would tell Grandma and Grandpa Bennett what they were doing to their baby-doll granddaughter.

I knew I wouldn't do any such thing, so I sighed and did what I was supposed to.

I was cleaning table nine when Doug and Kenny came out of the back office, where they had their snack that my mother had made. They walked over to me.

"When will Mom be home, Rona?" Kenny asked me in a quivery voice.

Not soon enough, I thought, but I suddenly felt sorry for him. He was only six. "Hey," I said, "you're going to have so much fun at the Y you won't even want to come home."

"You really think so?" He didn't sound sure at all.

"I'm positive," I said.

"I'm glad you're here." He still didn't sound altogether happy, but I liked the feeling I got when he said that.

"There's Joey and Ralph and Mrs. Porter," Doug called. "Over here, Joey. Ralph!"

Mrs. Porter waved and headed for the take-out counter. She made some wild motions with her arms and framed some words with her mouth, but I couldn't figure out what she wanted and didn't have time to try. She always struck me as soft in the head, and I was glad my mother had chosen the Y over Mrs. Porter. Her little brats came over and stared at me.

I gave them a cold look. "What do you want?"

Joey piped up, "Gee, Rona, you look funny in those goggles."

I glared at those twerps and could have knocked their heads together. "Scram, you two. Can't you see I'm busy?"

Then my father's voice called out loud and clear. "Doug, Kenny! You'd better wait outside for Mr. Brody so you won't miss him."

Mrs. Porter, all two hundred pounds of her, pushed her way through the crowd, an arm raised over her head, waving four pickles she was holding for dear life.

"Here's something for everybody." Smiling as if she was delivering a Care Package to some hopeless waif, who had been waiting for it for two years, she lowered her arm and the kids bit their pickles.

"Doug, Kenny," my father said again, this time in a threatening tone. He had a big frown line between his eyes, and the eyes themselves looked as if they knew Mom would not approve of half-sours at this time of day and especially after her wholesome food. He managed to twist his mouth up a little at Mrs. Porter, so she wouldn't think he was angry at her, which he was. He pointed in the direction of the door and the kids left. Mrs. Porter didn't take any notice. For the first time that day, I smiled in relief.

I was supposed to stay until 4:00 when the big crush would be thinning out. At half past three I had my other spare second for the afternoon. It seemed I had been there a week.

"Rona, see what table four wants."

"Yeah, Sam."

Table four had three girl students.

"Can I help you?" I felt like a drip asking that. I mean, I wasn't standing there for my health.

"I'll have a hot pastrami on dark with mustard on one side and Coke. What will you have, Linda?"

Linda had to give it some thought. She was making the critical decision of her life. "I'll have the same. No, change that. Make mine on light with mustard on both and a Pepsi."

There's a girl who knows her own mind.

The third one decided she'd have tongue and swiss on a roll, half with mayonnaise and half with mustard and a Coke, too. No, she'd rather have a ginger—no, Coke.

I walked to the eat-in counter and opened my mouth to give it all to Al when I saw Paul Wallace come in.

My blood supply freaked out and I wished that my father had a private office out of town instead of a public store in our own neighborhood, where people can come in and take you by surprise.

Paul was now standing beside me at the take-out. I heard him order a couple of half-sours and then say, "Hey,

Rona, how about a poem for the sport page? Our eighth grade is playing Franklin Roosevelt next Saturday."

Ohmygosh! Why do these things happen to me? How can I handle all this at one time? Football poem! I threw him a sneer look, which must have registered as frantic.

"You know, a football pep poem so they'll win."

Stupid! He must think I'm stupid. How could I be practically ignoring Paul Wallace! "Sure . . . sure Paul. Of course I know what you mean. I'll have one tomorrow." Boy, I nearly blew that one. I would have made one up right then and there if he wanted.

He smiled. That is, I think he smiled.

Then I just stood there thinking how handsome he was, forgetting how horrible I must look to him, and also forgetting to give my order for table four.

"What's yours, Rona?" Al asked.

I looked at him with a blank face to match my brain.

Al is nice. He prompted me, "What did the three girls at table four want?"

"Two hot pastramis and a tongue and swiss."

"What kind of bread?"

"Uh . . . light, dark and a roll."

"Which for which?"

"Uh, well." I sputtered and was very aware that Paul was taking it all in. I decided to just say anything and if the orders weren't right, I'd pretend I thought they were.

Finally Paul got his half-sours and turned to go.

"See you, Rona."

I absolutely got palpitations. He remembered to say good-bye!

"Bye, Paul." I hoped the palpitations didn't show.

29

He left, but the tingling sensation hung on for a while.

When I brought the girls their orders, they dug in without even looking at their sandwiches and kept right on with their conversation. I could have brought chocolate yogurt with tomato sauce for all they would have known.

The next time I looked at the clock I had fifteen minutes to go. Some fun day. I wasn't sure what part of me was tiredest, my legs or my head. It didn't matter. I got ready to collapse when something inside my tired head reminded me of the only good thing about the job—the money. I stood up real tall and straight.

"Uh . . . where do I get food to take out?" I heard a boy's voice say.

I looked up. He was wearing a beanie, which I knew from being around the college for so long meant he was a freshman. I pointed to the take-out and he walked over. My father was behind the counter.

"I'll have a sub and a frappe."

Daddy closed his eyelids and when he opened them he was looking at me with a particular look that said, "We know this kid is new around here." Then Daddy pointed to the sign on the wall behind the counter. It says:

We do not make subs. We do not make pizzas.
We do not carry ice cream. In the interest of
clean air we do not stock cigarettes.
Corn beef? Tongue? Hot pastrami? Pickles?
That we have. Enjoy.

(no tipping)

Daddy didn't say a word to the boy. He has this feeling about Cooper's that everybody ought to know it's an unusual store. As a matter of fact, I got a kind of unusual feeling

30

when he had looked at me as if we were sharing something. For a second it made me feel that I had suddenly jumped ahead about ten years.

When I was ready to leave, he said, "Not bad. Not bad at all." Then he patted my head, a thing he hasn't done since I was a little kid. That nice feeling from before came back again. I hoped the look on my face told him so.

At 4:02 I was home and called up Sharon.

"How was it, Rone?"

"Gruesome." I gave her all the details, especially about Paul. "Shar, I can't get over how I could have thought of my job or anything else in the world when he himself was standing right there."

"Well, natch, Rone. A job is important."

Chapter 5

At 5:00 I took the pots out of the refrigerator and stuck them in the oven.

At 5:30 Doug and Kenny showed up and I stuffed them in the living room beside the T.V. so they could watch their favorite kiddie programs until my mother came home.

I was setting the table when my father came in.

"Dorothy?"

"She's not here yet, Daddy."

"Oh."

I thought I should say something. "It was real busy today, wasn't it?"

He made some kind of muffled remark and disappeared into the bedroom.

By six o'clock my mother still didn't show. About every five minutes or so Daddy would put his head outside the bedroom door and say, "Dorothy?" or "I thought I heard the bell" or "Was that the front door?"

He even asked me if everything was okay in the kitchen and did I need any help. I told him I was managing, but actually I thought we sure were going to have baked shoe-leather for dinner if that stuff didn't get out of the oven soon.

At half past six my stomach was gurgling, and the kid-die programs were over. My mother still hadn't come home and my father was going bananas.

It was a quarter to seven when my mother turned the key in the door and practically fell on our broadloom.

"Dorothy!" My father ran to catch her as if he was some kind of circus performer and she was being thrown from the high wire.

The three of us kids stood stock-still while we watched to make sure my mother was all right. As soon as we knew she was, my father relaxed to the inside of his bones. Then he roared at Mom.

"Where were you and why didn't you call?"

You know how people react after they've been very worried about something and then find out that everything is okay.

Mom looked awful. I wasn't sure whether she was going to yell back or have a quiet-type tantrum. "I was out with clients. How could I leave them?"

"Thanks to Alexander Graham Bell we have the mod-ern convenience of the telephone."

"There is no such convenience present on Common-wealth Avenue between Berkeley and Clarendon Streets."

She turned to us kids and gave us a quick once-over to

33

make sure we weren't missing any arms or legs. Then she wanted the highlights of our day.

"Kenny, darling, did you go swimming?"

Naturally, he was the first one she was interested in. Chances are, Doug would be next on the list.

"Dougy, you played basketball? How many baskets did you make?"

"Four, Mom. Four!" He started dribbling an imaginary ball and aiming for an imaginary basket, and I'm sure he imagined he scored.

"Rona, I thought about you at two o'clock this afternoon."

Well, how nice. How long did the thought last, I wondered. I noticed she hadn't given Doug or Kenny any time limit on her thinking about them.

"Arnie, I'm sure Rona came through with flying colors." If her confidence in me showed on her face, I couldn't tell because I wasn't looking.

Before my father could contradict her statement, she was in the kitchen making like a homemaker. We finally got to the table and nobody, even my monster brothers, could get enthusiastic about the food on our plates, which my mother called lamb stew when she made it. Being overheated for two hours, it had lost its eye appeal, and after the first taste we knew the flavor was rotten.

My mother, of course, wasn't going to let on how bad it was, because she knew my father would say, "See!"

"Mom, this doesn't taste good. Why did you let Rona make it?" That was from Doug, as usual talking with food in his mouth, which made the insult even more disgusting.

I sort of nudged him under the table with my foot.

"Mom," he started to scream.

I wouldn't look at him, and my father told him to be quiet. Then Daddy asked Mom, "How was your day, Dorothy? Did you enjoy it?"

Her face lifted up. "Oh, very much. I had one lady from England and two from Australia in the group. It was wonderful. They told me they have nothing like this in their countries. All their sight-seeing is done by bus with none of the personal touch that we have."

I swear Daddy look disappointed. "I'm glad it was wonderful," he said. "But you are tired, aren't you?"

"Of course I'm tired," she answered. "It's only my first day. I have to get used to the schedule."

"Will your schedule include coming home at this hour every night and having us eat delicious food like this? Or shall we have a diet of corn-beef sandwiches for our nightly repast?"

"Arnie, you're being unfair."

I got tired turning my head from Mom to Daddy as if I was watching a tennis match. I got up to take my plate off the table and bring in the mess that my mother made for dessert. It had started out as her heavenly Indian pudding and ended up looking like burned walnut shells.

On my way to the kitchen I happened to look at our dining-room window and saw my face in the glass. I got scared white. I had forgotten about my handicap. Particularly since neither my mother nor my father had brought up the subject of how the Horace Mann School responded to my new image today. As far as they were concerned I could have been wearing those things all my life. My ugly glasses on my ugly face. If crying would help, I thought, I would cry a bathtub full or enough to fill up the Grand Canyon or the Atlantic and Pacific Oceans put together or . . . .

"Rona, while you're in the kitchen, would you bring in some more milk?"

How, I thought, can people in my family think about food when their only daughter has a severe problem tearing at her very soul? My mother's problem was a simple matter of schedule juggling; mine had deep-rooted complications.

I brought in the dessert and the milk and slumped down in my chair. I couldn't even put the so-called pudding on my spoon. I couldn't concentrate on my misery either because of all the hubbub with Doug and Kenny working at who could talk the loudest.

"Mom, Mr. Brody says I'm almost ready to be in the advanced beginners' group," Kenny proudly announced in a voice that must have been equal to ten million decibels.

In between those noises, words like "take-out," "eat-in" and "paid customers" bounced off my brain. My parents. All they cared about was that smelly delicatessen. The phone rang. "I'll get it." I jumped up, glad for a reason to get away from there.

"Rone." It was Sharon. "Through eating?"

"Just about."

"Uh . . . how do you feel?"

"Punk."

"Gonna watch T.V.?"

"I don't know."

"Did you write the football poem yet?" I guess she was trying to keep the conversation going until I'd feel better.

"I wrote it before dinner."

"The whole thing?"

36

"Sure."

"Gee, you write that stuff fast, Rone."

I shrugged my shoulders. Big deal. Then I said, "Well, call me if you think of any ideas about—well, you know." I couldn't come right out and say "raising money," with my parents in the next room.

But she knew of course what I was talking about. "Course," she said.

We hung up.

I dragged myself back to my slavery in the kitchen, sighing all the way. My mother was so tired she just plopped on the living-room sofa, and she and Daddy weren't having their usual type of conversation. Well, neither was I all that happy. But at least I could be alone with my private thoughts, awful though they might be.

I wished I were gorgeous, with beautiful eyes and curly blonde hair that would win me a prize—.

"Oh!" I let out a yell. I dropped the sponge in the sink and ran to the telephone. Then I realized my hands were wet so I ran back, dried them and flew back to the phone.

"Everything all right, Rona?"

"Yeah, Mom. I've got to call Sharon."

She was so used to that, she didn't say anymore.

"Shar, Shar," I screamed into the phone. "I've got it!"

"Whatja come up with?" she screamed back.

I was just about to tell her and stopped in time. I'd have to be very careful to get the idea across without giving it away at my end.

"Well." I cleared my throat a couple of times.

"Your folks there?"

"Mmm," I said.

"Well, give me some hints."

"Say, Sharon," I said in a different voice, "you know that football poem I wrote?"

"The one you just wrote so fast?"

"Yes," I said in the same voice, "I do a lot of those, you know."

"Right, you do." She just wasn't getting it, and I was having a fit because I was dying to tell her right out that the way I could earn money would be to write a million verses and sell them to the Happy Day Greeting Card Company right here practically in our neighborhood.

"Oh, Rone, give me a better clue," she wailed into the phone. "I'm sure I'll get it."

"Well, Sharon, people earn money doing that—and fast —and more than they could get doing other things and . . . ."

"Rone!" Her shriek went right to my eardrum. I knew she got it.

"You mean the Happy Day Greeting Card Company on Harwich Road?"

"Yes." I was trying to keep my voice normal, but I was going crazy inside.

"When? How? What will you write about? Tell me quick. I can't wait."

"People have birthdays, you know."

"Oh Rone, and anniversaries, and get married and have babies. Oh, Rone, you'll be a millionaire. You could be the poet laureate of Horace Mann School, of our whole town, our state. In fact, it could start you on your own literary career."

"Who's thinking of being a poet laureate?" I was hearing the jingle of money. All I could think about was how fast I could get the cash for the contacts.

"Rone, you know you stick a bunch of them in a folder, and that's called a portfolio. I know because my cousin—"

"Hey, Shar, I have to go." I had a blissful smile to match the way I was feeling. I wanted to get started. "I've got a lot of work to do tonight."

"Oh, right. See you in the morning, Rone. Wow!"

"Yeah. Wow, all right."

Because I had this secret knowledge of how I was going to earn private millionaire money, I could manage without getting upset at all about my icky brothers behaving like animals, or my parents arguing, or my having to do the dishes.

I moved back into the kitchen. Dark blue would be dreamy. No, violet is the color, a limpid violet. That's how writers describe the eyes of movie actresses—limpid. "Faye Dunaway appeared in an evening gown of shimmering silver sequins, a perfect complement to her limpid violet eyes." Ooh, the vision of those eyes gave me absolute chills.

Chapter 6

I worked like mad that night and when I met Sharon the next morning on the way to school, I had six greetings written in my spelling notebook. I started them on the page under the word list beginning with *constabulary* and ending with *coronation*. Our teacher's aide, Miss Bryant, is on some kind of English kick. She's majoring in British history, so we get a lot of fallout from her personal homework. Actually, I tried to fit those words into my poems. I couldn't do a thing with *constabulary*, but *coronation* reminded me of *crown*, and I used that in one of the Mother's Birthdays.

"How did you do?" Sharon asked me.

"Two Mother's Birthdays, three Get Wells, and a Happy Valentine," I reported.

"Let's see."

I showed her.

"Great, great, terrif, marvy, great! Rone, do about six more and we can get it to them real fast. Do you have a folder?"

"Get one for me at the stationery store. I have some money left over from my allowance."

"I'll bring it at four o'clock when you're through work, and we can bike over to Happy Day."

"Okay."

Then she remembered what I had told her about our family mess the night before and asked if I had to go home first and do something about dinner.

"No. My mother is trying something different tonight. The menu is going to be Colonel Sander's finger-lickin' fried chicken, which she'll pick up on her way home.

"Great."

"Well, not really. My father doesn't enjoy licking his fingers from anything except my mother's cooking."

"Oh-oh. Another family mess tonight."

I groaned in agreement.

"Will you be able to write all six poems today?"

"Like a breeze." I figured I could get half of them done by the time school was out.

Since in our first period we were supposed to write a composition on "My Ideal Way to Spend a Summer," I was sure I could fake it. I put a piece of paper on top of my composition sheet and after a couple of seconds in deep thought, I came up with a Welcome Baby Dear verse and started writing a mile a minute.

"Rona, you seem so enthusiastic writing your composition, I'm sure we'd like to hear it when you've finished."

Mrs. Holmes was standing two desks away smiling as if my enthusiasm was going to inspire the whole class to write plays like William Shakespeare. I convinced myself that she thought I was writing about my ideal summer but if I really had to read my Welcome Baby Dear poem, it might break up the class and not go across too well with Mrs. Holmes. I sort of nodded and put the verse paper in my desk.

I know I had a lot of nerve to think I could get away with doing anything besides math in math, but I tried.

"How many angles are there in a hexogram, Rona?"

I pulled my head up from "Baby Dear, we're glad you're here."

"Hexogram?"

"If we're interrupting something else you're doing, Rona . . . ." Mr. Curtis, our math teacher, thought he was being smart. I never *did* like him.

That was the end of my undercover work for the morning.

Being keyed up about earning the money for contacts kept me from feeling miserable about the reason for wanting them, until gym period.

There were about twelve of us from Mrs. Holme's class lined up for the high jump. Some of the kids were great, and some couldn't even get over a pole three inches off the ground. But I didn't care about that. What bothered me was, suppose my glasses fall off and I land on them and get cut to smithereens? What if I can't see while I'm in motion and fall on my head? What if . . . .

It was my turn. I automatically put my hand to where the bows join the frame to make sure they were on solid.

Janet Currier, who had already jumped and was coming off the mat, noticed. She sort of laughed. Well, it sounded more like a sneer. I was looking straight ahead and wouldn't let on that I'd heard her, but it hurt me to the quick.

I jumped. It was an ordinary height and I didn't fall or lose my glasses, but I felt sore. As if I *had* cut myself to smithereens over broken glass. Then Janet had to say to me right then, "Rona, if you wore contacts you wouldn't have to worry so much. My cousin Margi, who's sixteen, has them and they stick like *glue*."

Sixteen, and still needs them! That meant braces *and* glasses when I'd be sixteen! It took me two whole periods to get over it. But then what happened when the bell rang at 1:30 was so bad I can't imagine any other event in my whole life being worse. Even worse than my troubles so far.

Paul Wallace asked me to be on his editorial staff. My dream come true! But I just stood there looking like a dummy and feeling numb. Do I want to be on his staff? Do I want to breathe? Do I want contacts? Yes, I want to breathe, and yes I do want contacts as much as I want to breathe. For me to get contacts I have to work during those hours when the editorial staff has its very important meetings. Therefore, I cannot accept this once-in-a-lifetime offer. It has come into my life at the wrong time.

All this thinking took a lot of time during which Paul was being very brave standing there, waiting for an answer. Finally, I opened my mouth and shut it again. I could not come right out and say no.

"Well, do you want it?" he asked again.

"Yes, I do, Paul," I answered. But then I had to tell him, "Course I'm working after school now, you know, so . . . ."

"Oh yeah, that's right." He knew, all right. Hadn't I made a fool of myself yesterday afternoon with him looking on?

"Well," he said and shrugged his shoulders. A couple of his friends showed up, so he said good-bye and they walked off.

I was ready for the grave.

Sharon had been a witness to all this and we both felt so down about the whole thing, we didn't say a word to each other all the way to the deli.

When I came in the store I started right in with the pickle tray relay, only this time there were also a couple of coleslaw trays, too. I guess they figured I was experienced, by now. It was a good thing I had a lot to do, so I didn't have time to brood over my latest misfortune.

The place was as packed as the day before, but I was less limp because I was concentrating on my art. At about three o'clock I was going great, in my mind, on a Father's Day card. The thing went:

> Daddy dear, you work all year—
> you do it just for us.
> For you today, we shout hurray
> and

I was struggling for the punch line as I handed table six his ham on rye. Then it came to me and I said out loud, "Make a great big fuss."

The college-boy customer must have thought I was crazy.

"Who?" he asked.

"Who what?" I asked back. Boy, what a conversation.

"Who makes a big fuss?" I knew I was too far behind

44

in my orders to explain. So I clutched.

"Everyone makes a fuss—I mean no one. I don't know. I was talking to myself." If he didn't think I was crazy before, by now he was convinced.

"Hi Jerry. We see you found the place." Phew! Saved by the ham-on-rye's two friends. They sat down and were ready to order.

"We'll have our usual," ordered the tall one. I was beginning to realize why some waitresses have a nasty disposition.

"Well?" the jerk asked. He looked up at me with a dumb smile on his face.

"Well what? I don't know what your usual is?"

"Come on Jim, the kid's busy," the third one said. That was a relief.

"Okay Cliff, hot pastrami - on - pumpernickle - double - order - of - pickles - coleslaw - potato - salad - and - a- large coke. Twice." That was Jim, talking faster than I could listen, much less remember. Before I could get even madder and shove a pickle up Jim's nose, Cliff repeated the order slowly.

A few minutes later I brought table six their "usual," and Jim and Cliff studied the plates. Now what? I couldn't have handled any more grief.

"Thanks," Cliff said finally, with a smile. "It looks great." I felt better.

"Rona, order for table nine ready." I went off, and didn't see the boys leave.

By four o'clock I had only two greetings done, which meant I'd be handing in just nine altogether.

"Shar," I said when we were walking home to get our

bikes, "do you think they'll take only nine?"

"Course," she said. "You'll tell them it's just a sample of your work."

My work. That had a nice ring to it and gave me a certain feeling—*exalted* was the word that came to my mind. Which was funny, because *exalted* is kind of a religious word, and I don't think that writing greeting cards is a particularly religious act.

We went to my house and I copied down the verses neatly, one on a sheet, and put them in the folder. Then we got my bike from our basement storage place and went to Sharon's to get hers. We did not talk about Paul. I was going to have to put that subject completely out of my consciousness.

It's about a fifteen-minute bike ride to the greeting-card company, and scary waves kept coming over me the closer we got. Even thinking about my "work" didn't help.

The place looked like a big old-fashioned house with lots of grass and flowers around it. We parked our bikes and after just two steps up to the big porch, I got cold feet.

"Shar, I can't."

"You can."

"I'm scared."

"Think about the contacts."

"Oh, I'll do anything to get those contacts—anything."

"Well then, move."

"But I can't do this."

"All right, Rona Cooper. You're the one who can't live without contacts. Make up your mind. Either move, or stay stuck with those thick, thick—"

"I'm coming."

We pushed the front door open and walked into a big lobby that had a lot of potted plants and fancy rugs on the floor and weirdo paintings on the walls and a receptionist's desk. Two men were sitting on leather chairs flipping through magazines. I felt as if I was in a dentist's waiting room.

I noticed one of the men looking Sharon up and down as if she was twenty years old. Then I guess he realized she wasn't even a teenager, so he went back to his magazine.

"May I help you girls?" The receptionist was no Cathy.

I wasn't in any condition to tell her how she could help us, and Sharon got a rare case of shyness and didn't open her mouth either.

The girl gave us a hard look and this time said, "Is there something you want?"

I know that Sharon and I had our own idea about the answer to that question, but we still weren't saying anything out loud.

"If you're selling Girl Scout Cookies, we don't buy them, so . . . ." She was sort of dismissing us.

Sharon got her nerve up. "My friend has some greeting-card poems." Her voice sort of weakened by the end of the sentence. She motioned for me to give the creep the folder. I laid it on her desk.

She looked at it as if it was an abandoned cat left on somebody's back doorstep. "We do not accept unsolicited manuscripts in that form," she sniffed.

"How . . . uh . . . which way is it supposed to be?" I asked her wondering what *unsolicited* meant.

"It has to have a stamped, self-addressed return envelope.

"Oh," I said. Sharon was too speechless to speak.

"If you live around here you can bring it back tomorrow with the envelope."

"Sure, thanks."

We left.

"Boy," I snorted, when we got to our bikes. "She really intimidated us. I don't know why we let her. I don't *like* to be intimidated."

"Should we come back tomorrow and not let her intimidate us?"

I let out a deep breath. "No, I'll buy two envelopes and we can get to the P.O. before it closes and send it right out now. I'm not too interested in seeing her again."

We rode a little way. "You don't have to come if you don't want to, Shar."

"Of course I'll come. We're going to see this thing through."

We saw it through the mail shute, and I looked at the slit in the wall with small hope and a big prayer. "Let's get out of here," I said.

"Listen Rone, I would say that those nine verses will bring in around—well, I'll bet around forty-five dollars at least. I mean, how can they give you less than five dollars apiece?"

"Easy. They can give me nothing."

"You're not supposed to feel that way. You've got to hang in there, Rone."

All I did was feel sorry for myself in advance.

When we got to my house, Sharon said, "Well, Ah hope your frahed chicken is fingah-lickin' good."

I made a face to show I wasn't looking forward to it.

"See you tomorrow, Shar."

I unlocked the door, glad to be home before Doug and Kenny. The less time I had to spend with them today, the better.

I heard a cough coming from my parents' bedroom, then the dial sound from the phone in there. If the robber was making a call, I definitely was not going to surprise him. I didn't budge. I couldn't.

"Arnie?" It was my mother's voice, very full of sore-throat sound. "I'm glad I got you before you left."

I went to the doorway. She was in her nightgown and robe, under the covers in bed. Her fingers waved a weak hello. I just stood there looking and listening.

"Arnie, I had to come home early. I have a terrible cold . . . I don't *know* how I got it, but Charlotte thought I should leave . . . Yes, Arnie, I thought I should too . . . Arnie, I didn't feel up to shopping, so you'd better bring some corn-beef sandwiches for supper . . . Arnie, I don't feel well—please!"

I had a pretty good idea of what my father must have said.

For a second I wondered if I was going to have to sub for my mother as a tour guide, too.

Chapter 7

When my father came home that night, he was what I think is called livid. His mouth was a stiff line across his face. His nostrils looked angry and his eyes weren't exactly warm and loving, which they ordinarily would have been with my mother sick.

Usually at the first sign of even a sneeze from her he gets very maternal and starts with, "Take some aspirin, Dorothy" and "Don't come into the store tomorrow, honey, you need a rest" and a lot of stuff like that. She usually answers with, "Arnie, don't baby me, I'm all right," and then she'll kiss him on his bald spot. They are, on the whole, a very loving couple.

But this time, with my mother really sick, my father was in quite a different form. He stood in the bedroom doorway with his arms wrapped around three big brown-paper bags filled with goodies from Cooper's Deli. Nobody, unless they had what my father calls a full-blown cold, could miss what was in those bags. It was the drive-you-crazy, fresh-rye-bread, spiced-meat and pickle smell.

In the meantime the boys were home and they almost tore off my father's jacket to get at the food. He was in such a bad mood he jerked the top of his body away from them and kept glaring at my mother. Not a word passed between them for fully ten seconds. Then the dialogue that followed wasn't exactly tender or friendly. Mrs. Daniels seemed to be the outstanding thing that bothered my father.

"Your boss told you to go home?" he asked.

It wasn't so much the words themselves but the inflection. If he had used that pitch of voice on me, I would have shivered.

"She is not my boss and furthermore, Arnold Cooper, neither are you," my mother croaked at him.

He ignored the remark.

"So, because you are nobody's slave, your husband and children have to survive on cold cuts. And also because you're nobody's slave you work two days and take to your bed."

"Arnie, we'll discuss it when I'm better."

"Dorothy, tell me, did you ever get sick from two days' work in the store, even with the dirty college kids?"

No answer.

He raised his voice, "Did you?"

My mother blew her nose, fell back on the pillow and moaned, "Go away, Arnie. You're liable to catch whatever I have. Go eat, and leave me alone."

We ate, but outside of the two younger male members

51

of the clan, we didn't enjoy the taste as much as the smell.

The next day, although my mother's health improved, the air in our house was slightly polluted with my father's remarks about "reordering priorities" and my mother's about "getting a new viewpoint" or total silence. All I did was try to keep out of their way.

By Sunday afternoon my mother was well enough to plan to go back to the tour job the next day.

"You sure you feel okay, Mom?" I asked her, imagining the revolution there'd be in my house if she konked out again.

She told me she felt great but she would just as soon not mention it to Daddy until the next morning. The next morning he was just as upset as he would have been the night before. Of course there was a shorter number of hours that my mother had to feel Daddy's disapproval. But if it was me I'd have told him sooner, so that by the time next morning came he'd have been more used to it and I could go to work without all that steam.

I was in the store at my regular time that afternoon, when I saw Jerry, Cliff and Jim coming in.

"Over here," I yelled to them, pointing to table six. I waited till they came, so I could take their orders, and that was when I got the shock of my life.

Jerry was walking with a white cane. He was blind! I nearly died on the spot. How could I not have noticed before?

They sat down and I just stared. I guess I was stupified.

"Rona," he said. Now that I knew, it sounded partly like a question. After all, he wasn't really sure it was me. And he remembered my name!

"Hi, Jerry," I said. I wondered if I sounded self-conscious.

"I'm starving," Jim said. I barely heard him. All I could think about was Jerry. I tried to tell them about the great Romanian pastrami and potato pancake special of the day. But my head kept ringing. I had never seen a blind person before, and I had the strangest sensation looking at Jerry.

The three of them wanted the special, and I was in a kind of daze when I walked over to the counter to put in their order. It would take about ten minutes because the pancakes are made up fresh, so I went back to see if they wanted anything in the meantime.

"Do you want something while you're waiting?" I looked at Jim and Cliff. I thought it would be too obvious to look at Jerry, so I deliberately kept my eyes away from him.

"If you turn toward me, Rona, I can hear you better," I heard Jerry say. I nearly jumped, then turned to look at him.

"With this din in here, you have to speak fairly loudly, because I can't read lips, you know." He smiled a little.

Now I noticed his eyes. I could see the difference. The difference was there was no expression in them. The happy or sad look that you see in people's eyes wasn't there. They were sort of blank. All the happy or sad looks he would have would show mostly around his mouth.

Golly, he talks about his affliction as if it doesn't bother him at all. And then, strangely, just like that, his blindness didn't seem so awful to me. Maybe because of his personality. He was so comfortable to be near. As a rule, I think,

53

if you hear about a handicap like that but don't see it, it bothers you more than if you're face-to-face with it.

"Want some free half-sours while you wait?" I asked.

"Sold!" Cliff said.

When I brought the pickles, they had their notebooks open and were talking about some stuff written in them.

I wondered about Jerry's notebook. I sneaked a look at it and saw that the pages were of heavier paper than those in regular notebooks. They were tan-colored without lines and covered with raised dots. He was running his fingers over the dots, which must have been some kind of a code, because I could tell he was getting something out of it. Braille. I remembered the word. That's what Braille looks like.

Jerry was saying to the others, "And he'll probably ask us how to find the functions of the different regions of the cerebral cortex..."

First I felt surprised that he sounded so smart. Then I was surprised that I was surprised. Jim grabbed a pickle and started crunching.

"Ah, the pickles," Jerry said, feeling for the plate. I reached out to move it toward his hand.

Cliff pulled my hand away, shaking his head. I guessed if I had moved the plate in front of them it would make Jerry feel he couldn't find the pickles himself. I was still wobbly in the head seeing how well he managed.

"I'll go check on your pancakes," I said.

On the way back to the counter I took a couple of more orders from some people. I was getting pretty good at remembering orders, and I was managing smiles practically as good as Cathy.

"Hi, Rona, take my table next." And "over here, Rona," a bunch of customers were calling.

Gee, people know me. I forgot to be afraid of them. I got the most terrific feeling. People liked having me wait on them. I do think that when people like you it makes whatever you're doing better.

A crazy thought came into my head. I couldn't possibly take the job with Paul because then I couldn't be around this bunch. For the short time that thought was in my head, I didn't even remember about the contacts.

I brought the panakes to table six. "How's that for service?" I said, feeling practically cocky.

"If you keep this up, we'll have to be your regular customers," Cliff said.

I didn't object to that at all.

As they left and I watched them working their way out to the door, I was very impressed that nobody looked at Jerry as if he was something unusual.

When I was getting ready to leave for the day, I was quite surprised that I didn't even want to go. It was the first time I had actually enjoyed working in Cooper's Deli.

"Rona, don't forget to pick up your envelope before you go home," my father called out to me, almost smiling. Maybe he was getting used to my mother's stand-in.

"What envelope, Daddy?"

"You've forgotten so soon? Your bonus package." He watched my reaction.

I beamed. I felt that shafts of sunshine came jutting out of me. "Ooh, I can hardly wait to count it."

"So what are you going to do with all your money?" Al had been listening.

I blushed.

"Oh, pick up a couple of things I've been wanting." I hoped I sounded casual.

When Daddy gave me the envelope, I almost ripped the money taking it out. Ten crisp dollar bills. I separated them and turned them over in my hands and smoothed my fingers over them. I counted them four times before I finally put them carefully back in the envelope, and my head was swimming.

Ten dollars. How very, very gorgeous. Ten dollars toward the purchase of the most important thing in the world. I was going to be transformed from ugly duckling to lovely swan with one choice pair of contacts. What a beautiful day this was.

Sharon was outside waiting for me.

"Shar, the most superperfect thing."

"Somebody left you a thousand-dollar tip."

"No, you know that's against rules."

"Uh, one of the customers sells black-market contacts and he fell for you and will give you a pair free."

"Shar, you don't have to guess. I'm *telling* you. I got paid! Real money!"

"Oh Rone, how fab! How much? Lemme see!"

"I just happen to have on me the gigantic sum of ten U.S. Treasury dollars, and if you play your cards right, I might let you look."

"Rone, Rone," Sharon was jumping up and down like crazy. "Lemme see, lemme see!" She was positively squealing.

You'd think neither one of us had ever seen United States currency before. I took out the bills from the envelope, one by one, by the tips of my fingers and fanned them in front of her face. "These, Sharon Simmons, are genuine, fresh-from-the-mint American greenbacks to be used toward the purchase of two exquisite purple-colored contacts for one Rona Cooper, future razzle-dazzle girl of the Horace Mann School." I took a bow.

"Purple, Rone? I like sea-green."

"Purple it is, Miss Simmons. Exotic is what we are going to be—exquisitely exotic."

Then finally Sharon got more natural and so did I.

"Hey, Shar, a fantastic thing happened today in the store."

"Besides getting paid, you mean?"

"Yeah. One of the college boys that I waited on is blind."

"Ooh Rone." She squeezed up her face.

"Yeah, but Shar, it's so strange. I mean, he's like regular. You'd never know."

"Does he wear dark glasses?"

"No. The first time I saw him I had no idea."

"Does he have a Seeing Eye dog?"

"No, he uses a cane. A white one with a red stripe on it."

"And he goes to college! How does he do his homework?"

"With Braille. You know those dots they feel with their fingers. And they can read what it says. Shar, he's so smart, you should hear him talk."

"Do you think he goes out with girls and things?"

"I don't know. He eats at our deli with a couple of his boyfriends."

"Gee, I wonder . . . ." She frowned wondering about it all. I wondered too, but not as much because I knew first-hand how like everybody else he is.

Chapter 8

When my mother came home that evening she was all out of breath but pretending to be full of pep as she bustled off to get dinner ready. Daddy was still mad, so in self-defense she was using me as the middleman to relay messages to him. She used this technique even when we were all present at the same place.

"Rona, you might tell your father," she said as we started to eat, "that during my lunch hour today I went over to Berger's Fish Market to get him some finnan haddie for tomorrow night's dinner, which I shall prepare tonight the way he likes it." The idea there being that she was going to show him she could handle all her responsibilities with no sweat.

Before I could pass on the message my father got into the act. "Rona, tell your mother I don't like my tomorrow night's meal of my favorite or any other recipe prepared twenty-four hours in advance of my eating it."

I hate being dragged into their arguments like that. Thank heavens it doesn't happen often.

Doug looked at my father and mother as if he just lost his marbles. Then he caught on, he thought. With a mouthful of hamburger that my mother had bought on her way home, he said, "Oh, this is a game. Who can I have for my partner to tell things through?"

Now loudmouth joined in. "Can we whisper too, besides talking out loud?" That was a gem—whispering Kenny Cooper. When he brings his voice down to a yell, my mother's imported crystal cracks.

"Doug, try, try real hard to finish chewing and swallowing before speaking." My mother, I am sure, was glad she had a good reason not to have to answer his question about the "new game."

"Kenny, if you don't split my eardrums before you're sixteen, then it only means my eardrums are indestructible." I am sure my father was glad he had an excuse too.

I was glad when dinner was over.

The next morning my mother gave me my food-preparation instructions for the day. "Take the casserole of finnan haddie out of the refrigerator the minute you get home so it will warm up gradually."

"Okay, Mom." I got the funny feeling that even though she wanted us to think she found her new career challenging and glamorous, she would much rather stay home and please Daddy than take off on those walking tours.

After school Sharon reminded me it was almost a week since we mailed the stuff to Happy Day Company.

"Rone, maybe you should stop by your house on your way to the store to see if any mail came from them."

"No. I'd rather be uncertain and hope."

But right after work I ran home. When I got to the hall of my building, I looked through the slit opening of our mailbox. It was packed with mail, and I was sure my brown envelope from Happy Day was there. *An acceptance!*

I ran upstairs like a shot and zoomed in the front door. My mother was home already.

"Hi, Mom. You're home early. You look wonderful. Absolutely radiant." I hugged her.

"Why all the bubbly? Did you come into some scholarship money?" She sure worried a lot about our college tuition.

"That's not till next year, Mom. You have to wait until seventh grade to apply to college. But don't you worry, Mom, with both of us working, we'll take care of Cooper tuitions all the way."

"Why the joy-to-the-world?" she asked again.

"Oh, I don't know, Mom. Everything's just great."

"Working in Cooper's definitely has agreed with you."

It does agree with me, I thought. It was just so great meeting people like Jim and Cliff and Jerry. Especially Jerry. And it was great, too, having people glad to see me and liking what I could do for them. And it was earning money for a very special, vital cause, which reminded me. "The mail came, Mom. I'll go down and get it and be back in a jiff."

I pulled the mailbox key from the hook by the door and skimmed down the stairs without waiting for the pokey elevator. As I pushed the key in the lock, my hand was vibrating to match my heartbeat. There were three envelopes inside.

One was from the telephone company. One was a letter from the Earthenware Crockery Company, which was probably a bill for the new dishes Daddy ordered bearing the Cooper seal. He had answered an ad that said they'd look up your family escutcheon. Daddy knew darn well the Coopers never had a coat-of-arms, but we thought it would be a good gag and Daddy said it would add class to the deli.

I fumbled in the mailbox for the large envelope. There it was! The brown envelope addressed to me in my handwriting. I tore it open

"Dear Contributor, the letter started, "Thank you for sending the enclosed material." They thanked me—they must like it!! The next sentence read, "We regret to inform you"—Dear God, it sounds like a next-of-kin-missing-in-action letter from the War Department—"this is not suitable for us and we are returning herewith."

I crunched the letter into a wrinkled ball. Somehow I managed to lock the mailbox. Then I moved my body toward the elevator without makng the effort to lift my feet. I pushed the elevator button. I mean, who was in a hurry?

Of course I've felt bad in my life. I have had plenty of disappointments before. But never like this. Never. Frankly, there just didn't seem to be any reason to go on living. I could never attain my first ambition and would never have the desire for my second.

I've got to call Sharon, I thought.

Mrs. Miranda, the neighbor on top of us, came in the front door with some groceries.

"Hello, Rona. Been waiting long?"

I didn't remember. "No," I said.

"You can wait forever for this thing."

"Mmm," I said just to make conversation.

"If I didn't live on the fourth floor, I'd never waste the time," she clucked away.

Finally the stupid thing came and we got on.

"Bye," I said at the third floor.

"Bye, Rona. Say hello to your mother."

I think that's a dumb expression. When I come in I'm supposed to say, "Hello, Mother."

"Okay, Mrs. Miranda, bye again." ·

"Bye, Rona." Thank heavens the door closed.

I was still clutching the wrinkled ball of rejection and the envelopes in my fist when I came back in our apartment. I put the other mail on the hall table.

My mother took one look at me. "What happened?"

How could I tell her?

"Rona, answer me. Are you all right?"

"I'm . . . okay." I managed to get that out but no more.

"Something is wrong. What is it?"

"N-nothing, Mom, honest." I certainly didn't want her getting suspicious about my extracurricular activities, which, naturally, I think every person has a right to keep private.

My mother's tone changed. "When I was your age," she informed me, but not for the first time, "I had no secrets from my mother."

I sighed. "Mom, today if a mother has to know everything that's going on with her daughter, it's called invasion of privacy."

"I am unmoved." She eyed my fist. "What's in the letter?"

Then I got real nervy. I said in a high and tight voice, "Mom, if I am old enough to work, I am old enough to read my personal mail without confiding or revealing the contents, and I don't want to talk about it."

I took long strides down the hall to the phone and dialed Sharon. I had my back to my mother so I wasn't sure which face she had on, but I heard her walk toward the kitchen.

"Shar," I fairly hollered into the phone. "Shar, I've got to see you. In person."

"I'll come right over."

"No," I told her. "Not here."

"Can you come here?"

"I think a neutral place would be better."

Mrs. Simmons is on friendly terms with my mother, and since I started this little feud with my mother I didn't want her to get information from Mrs. Simmons in case Sharon and I were overheard.

"Where?"

"The usual."

"Now?"

"Now." I hung up. "Mom, I have to see Sharon for a second," I called into the kitchen. "I'll be right back."

My mother made some sounds that I couldn't translate. My conscience bothered me, so I said, "I'll set the table and stuff, Mom. I'll be back in a second."

I ran down the stairs, out the front door, around the left corner to Buswell Street where Sharon was already waiting.

"What's up, Rone?"

"Shar, I'm going to die," I yelled, ending in a gasp like

the heroine in a T.V. program who's just been shot by the mob.

"Take it easy, Rone. Is it your folks?"

"No."

"No? What else is there?"

"Happy Day . . ." I couldn't finish the sentence.

"No!"

"Yes."

"Why? What'd they say?"

"No."

"Oh."

We both stood there looking at each other as if it was all over.Finally Sharon,who is a real organized,manager type of person, and a remarkable friend, said, "You will write some more."

"Shar, I can write that stuff in my sleep. That's not the problem."

"What's the problem?"

"The problem is that no matter how much of that junk I write, I guess it's just junk. So, no matter who I send it to, it's going to get sent back."

Sharon turned that over in her mind, then said, "Somebody, somewhere, can use your poetry. Let me think. Keep quiet, Rone, while I think."

I kept quiet.

"Rone," she said as if she was making an announcement from the stage of the school auditorium, "we will go to the library tomorrow and check out other greeting-card companies from a book they have there, and you will send your poems to them. Happy Day is not the only company on the map."

"Okay, Shar," I said, not feeling okay at all. "Tomorrow."

I slouched home. In my innermost soul I didn't feel that my meeting with Sharon, the manager, had amounted to anything real positive.

When I got in our building, I decided against the elevator. It was too boring just to stand there doing nothing. At the stairway I looked up the stairwell to the skylight in the roof, took a pretty big breath and started lifting one foot after the other.

What was I going to do? Really do. Contacts cost $200. I only had $10, my total wordly funds. I would have to write and have accepted thirty-eight verses, figuring $5 per verse.

But *have accepted* was the rub. By the time we'd find a company that would buy them, I'd have discouraged every living soul from looking at me, including Paul Wallace. Just thinking his name made me feel warm all over. There were only two more steps to the third floor. I stalled for a second, letting the warm feeling last. Then I got to my door and opened it.

My brothers were watching Mr. Rogers on T.V. I went in the kitchen to live up to my commitment about setting the table. My mother was standing in front of the stove staring into space with a look on her face as if she had just seen her home go up in flames. She sure took what I had said hard.

"Mom," I started to apologize. "I didn't mean it like I said it."

She looked at me and so far as I could notice, my apology made no impression. Her expression was still the same —she was very hurt.

Was what I said really so bad? Frankly, I didn't think I had to tell my mother every little thought, plan, or idea I had. Why did she have to feel so crushed? Did *she* tell her mother *everything* when she was my age?

"Rona, I'm very upset."

"I can see that, Mom, and I'm sorry. It wasn't really an important letter," I lied.

She gave me a kind of half smile, up on one side. "The letter . . .? Oh, the letter."

My poor mother. She's getting senile. I waited because I didn't know how to handle this situation.

"Rona, I have a confession to make."

Hah! She *didn't* tell her mother everything!

"I . . . I have to tell your father something and . . . and it's going to be very difficult for me." She plopped down on a chair.

I turned cold. She's going to leave him! Her need for independence is stronger than her love.

"Oh, Mom." I looked at her as if *I* saw the house go up in flames.

"Rona," she went on, "I've made a terrible mistake. A terrible mistake," she repeated, "and now I have to face it."

"What about us, Mom?" I wailed, wondering who was going to get custody. I had a passing thought that if there was going to be any separate awarding of children by the court, then I wanted to go with one parent and my brothers could have the other. But I was so overcome that I said, "We want both of you. Both you and Daddy."

My mother's expression changed. Radically. She looked at me as if *I* was going up in flames. "What are you talking about?"

"About the divorce, of course." That rhymed. Without even working at it I made up poems. Happy Day doesn't appreciate a natural artist.

"Whose divorce? Who's getting a divorce?"

"You and Daddy. Aren't you?"

"Dear God. What did he say to you?"

"He? You said." One of us was definitely crazy.

"Rona." She grabbed me by my shoulders and looked straight into the middle of those hideous circles. "Rona, let's start at the beginning." Then she spoke very slowly and clearly as if I was some kind of Neanderthal idiot. "What do you think I said about getting a divorce?"

"You said," I answered, "that you made a mistake and you had something to tell Daddy that was very difficult for you."

She kept looking at the exact same spot on my lenses while she realized what she'd said. Then she let go of me and sat down again and laughed until the tears came to her eyes. Absolutely hysterical. I figured she had something less drastic than a divorce on her mind, so I waited patiently for her to get through her little scene. After she wiped her eyes a couple of times, she finally simmered down. She got up and hugged me.

"Rona, sweetheart, I haven't felt so good in years. You don't know what a relief this is."

"It would be nice if you'd let me in on it." I said.

"Honey, I'm quitting working for Charlotte the end of next week, and I am permanently through with an outside job!"

"Quitting! Mom, I thought you were crazy about walking!"

68

'I am, honey, I am." Her eyes were still shining and full of twinkle.

"Well? Didn't you like meeting those interesting people and getting out in the real world?"

"Rona," she said with an expression I'd never seen on her face before, "The deli is the real world for me."

"Then there's nothing to worry about, Mom."

"Your father."

"What do you mean, my father?"

"I have to save face, Rona. Your father will lord it over me for the rest of my life that he was right and I shouldn't have taken the job in the first place."

"Daddy wouldn't do that, Mom. He'll be so glad to have you back in the store, he'll . . . ." Then I remembered. "Ooh," I groaned. My job! My own mother was going to take away my only source of income!

"What's the matter, honey?"

"You . . . you'll go back to the deli, huh?"

After a second she said, "Rona, you're a genius!"

She couldn't have been reading my mind because what I'd been thinking was definitely not of genius quality. Frankly, I had a pure fear of competition. My father, maybe after a few laughs, would welcome his wife back to the store and presto—curtains for me.

"Oh, darling, you've made it so clear," she went on, working out her plot. "I tell Daddy I've quit Charlotte's company out of the goodness of my heart because I see how you all, mostly he, have been suffering. And I will tell him that I firmly believe my place is in the home. Then he will beg me to come back to the store, and I will allow myself to do so after three or four begs."

"How long do you think that will take?" I asked, trying to gauge how much money I could earn before she'd take my job away.

"Oh, not more than a week."

A week. That was only twelve more dollars.

"I'd let him do a few more begs if I were you, Mom. No sense in being too easy."

"Yes, working in the store has become quite attractive to me this week," my mother said.

It had for me, too.

"Rona, we'll just wait and see how it goes, won't we?" She smiled at me as if I was her partner in a bank-heist plan.

We heard the key in the lock.

"I'm home." Daddy was practically singing the announcement, putting an extra syllable in *home*.

Everybody gave him his hello hug, except my mother. They hadn't completely made up yet.

Daddy came over to her, gave her one of his own brand of nice looks and then they hugged and kissed.

Thank goodness.

"I am happy to state," he said with a fair-sized smile after the second kiss, "that as of a week from next Monday, a lovely young lady has been hired who will take over the duties of waitress and general aide in Cooper's Delicatessen."

Need I say? My mother and I looked at each other with unadulterated, devastated shock.

Chapter 9

Later my mother told me she wished she'd burned the finnan haddie.

I'm not sure if dinner that night was better or worse than the night they were using me as their go-between.

Mom, of course, was furious and didn't want Daddy to know it. She was also dying to find out who the girl was, how he found her and what she looked like. But she didn't want him to know that she cared.

Daddy was acting very nonchalant—he knew how Mom really felt and he was pretending that she was very pleased about the new arrangement. Now she could feel relaxed with her new job knowing he had an adult replacement for her and I wouldn't have to come into the store.

"Dorothy, I've been thinking. Why don't we have my mother come over to the house every afternoon to give the children a snack? Then they could be picked up here for the Y, instead of having to go to the store, and she could help get dinner ready. Wouldn't you feel easier about that while you're being a tour guide?"

Daddy's mother is not exactly my mother's favorite person. She's not all bad, but she's a little on the bossy side, and the whole idea would not sit well with Mom. Daddy knew that very well, too.

"Diabolical," my mother whispered to me when we went in the kitchen to get the dessert.

The picture was becoming very clear to me. Daddy was using strategy to get Mom to give up her job and come back to the way things used to be. So far as I was concerned, all I wanted was my job. I needed that money!

After dinner I went in my room and found it very hard to concentrate on our assignment to start a file on Unusual Events. I had one I could imagine happening right in my own life if I got desperate enough. I could just see the write-up in the newspaper:

> A sixth-grade Boston girl, caught holding up an optometrist's office, pleaded for mercy. "I did it for contacts," she cried. The police were at a loss to understand what she meant by that. Didn't she have enough contact with others in her school? Judge Jones sentenced the girl to 30 days hard labor.

I didn't sleep too well that night.

The rest of the week was a drag. I didn't even see Paul. Maybe he was sick. Trying to forget about my not being able to take his offer on the *Horn* wasn't working out. I thought about it a lot. What was I going to do? Take the job and not get contacts? And leave my customers in the deli? Or stay in the deli and not be on the staff with Paul? I bet the Queen of England doesn't have such hard problems to solve.

By the time Sunday arrived, I was exhausted and the kind of day it turned out to be didn't help build me up either. We had a houseful of relatives so I couldn't have one phone conversation. The relatives included Grandma Cooper, who shook her head as if we got invaded by the Russians, and said to Mom, "You certainly are undertaking a great deal, Dorothy. Are you sure it isn't more than you can handle?"

Mom smiled and didn't say anything. Then Grandma looked at me. Grandmothers, naturally, are always sweet and kind to their grandchildren, but that Sunday I felt worse and worse the nicer my grandmother acted. This was the first time she had seen me with my new apparatus.

"Rona, sweetheart, how would you like to come in town with me next Saturday and we'll go to lunch together? You know, the Blue Sail, the restaurant you love."

Ordinarily I would have been mad about the idea. Up to last week I would have accepted before she'd finish asking, but now I felt she was just pitying me. I couldn't.

"It must be months since we've had a day together, sweetheart. Grandma would love to get you a new dress, too. How about it?"

This bending over backwards and referring to herself in the third person the way adults do to a two-year-old was painful.

"Sure, Grandma." What else could I say? But I wasn't as excited as I usually get. I wondered if my personality was going to change along with my face.

My uncle and aunt on my father's side were there too. They have two kids, a boy and a girl ages fifteen and sixteen who, of course, didn't have to show up, since by the time you get that age you're set free from accompanying your parents everywhere. A remark from that side of the family to my mother was, "Dorothy, you must be so excited about your new job. I'll bet you wish you did it years ago!"

My father glared at his only sister and asked Uncle Jaimy to join him at the T.V. for the Dallas Cowboy-Miami Dolphin game.

They went into the other room and that left me for Aunt Betty. She eyed me as if I'd be safer in a cage and then said, "Well, Rona, how do you like working in the pickle factory?" At least she didn't ask me how much money I was earning.

"It's okay, Aunt Betty." I remembered my manners more than I felt them.

The relatives on my mother's side now trouped in. My Aunt Joyce looked at my glasses and said, "Dorothy, why don't you get retainers on her teeth and get the worst part of it all over with now?"

I felt like I was hit with a meat cleaver.

Aunt Lillian made her contribution directly to me, "Rona, dear, your eyes might change, honey, and in a few years you probably won't need glasses at all."

The "dear" and the "honey" didn't help one bit. I kept thinking, grown-ups sure don't know how to talk to kids, even in their own family.

I left for my bedroom with my five-year-old girl cousin and we played with her dolls. Which was an improvement over listening to that type of adult talk and a better choice

74

than going into one of my brother's bedrooms, where o
boy cousins, nine and seven, were tearing the room apa

The next morning while Daddy was shaving and I v
getting my detail for the day, I asked my mother, "Did y
tell him?"

"Not yet."

"Will Grandma be coming?"

"We are holding off on that decision until next wee

I felt like saying something optimistic but I was fee
too depressed about my own problem at the time.

"Have a nice day, Mom," was the best I could do.

"You too, honey," she sighed.

Sharon was waiting at Buswell.

"Rone, you look as if something even worse happer

"It did."

"What could?"

"I'm losing my job."

"How can your own father fire you?"

"He's not firing me. He's replacing me."

"Same thing, Rone. Your mother coming back?"

"Who knows?"

"What do you mean?"

I told her and finished up with, "And you know
going to cut me down to nothing."

"Well then," she said as if it was all settled. '
have to write . . . . Let's see, you made ten the first w
twelve last, so you need a hundred and seventy-eight
dollars a greeting, you'll have to write—"

"Thirty-five and a part of one," I said without
of emotion.

"You've been working on it, huh?"

"Yeah."

"Well, okay, if you do six a day that will be . . . ."

"Six days and one poem left over," I said with still no real life in my voice.

Trudy and Bev met us at the intersection of Ivy and St. Mary, so Sharon and I started another subject of conversation right away. Which was a big relief to me. The thought of six days and a portion of the seventh writing six poems a day suddenly seemed like the most uninteresting way possible to spend my time. If I did, I was sure they were all going to be condolence cards. In fact, the first one I'd write would be a Deepest-Sympathy-on-the-Loss-of-Your-Job poem.

I don't know how I got through that school day. I either answered everything wrong, didn't know the answer or didn't hear the question.

"Having an off day, Rona?" Mrs. Holmes asked me on the way out after the bell rang.

"I guess so," I said.

"Getting used to the new glasses takes a little time." She smiled. "I understand."

Did she now? Another one with a pretty face and nothing that she needed to help her see through. How could she understand? Nobody could understand. NOBODY. And with my parents creating a deprived home life for me, I felt as rejected as my poetry portfolio.

Sharon met me on the stairs.

"Do you have time now to go to the library or should we wait until after work?"

"Neither one," I snapped at her. "I am despondent. Utterly and completely and totally despondent. I can't write

any more poems. Nobody wants them, and I don't care anyway."

"You'd better care and you'd better write them too. Because if you don't get your purple contacts, you won't have the moral stamina to carry on."

"I do too have moral stamina, Sharon Simmons. What kind of a way is that to talk?"

"I am only trying to help and you aren't cooperating." Her voice became kind of shrill.

"You're right, I'm a rat," I shouted at her.

"Okay, rat, you can go to the library yourself or you don't have to go at all. It's your problem, Rona Cooper. Good-bye."

We were at the door. Sharon pushed it open and ran down the path to the street before I had a chance to make up or yell back. I didn't even care. So I've lost my best friend. What difference does anything make anyway?

I headed for the deli. All right, Rona, I said to myself, so what's the scoop now? I talk to myself sometimes because I have found it very helpful in sorting things out when they get confusing. I mentally work the problems around until they're straight. I don't move my lips or talk out loud, though. Bev Baker is a great one for that. Sometimes she even has a two-way conversation going, with herself taking both parts.

Anyway, I was answering myself mentally. You numbskull, I said, you just lost your best friend. Now who are you going to complain to about your financial problems? And who are you going to confide in about life in general? And who—

"Rona, you'll only have to do thirty-six!" It was Sharon's voice screaming.

I stopped where I was. She was halfway down the block, facing me and standing there.

"You'll be getting twelve more for this week and Saturday morning. So you subtract that and all you need is one sixty-six. And that makes only thirty-three poems and a part of one, making thirty-four."

"I thought you were mad at me," I yelled down the block.

For a second she didn't say anything. Then she yelled back, "I was and I am." After a couple more seconds she yelled, "But we're friends, aren't we?"

"Sure," I yelled back.

"Well, I can still be your friend and still be mad, that's all." She turned and ran around the corner out of sight.

I think Sharon and I will be friends even when we're real old. I felt good about that. But it didn't change anything else. Two less poems to write in six days was still no great bargain.

When I walked into Cooper's Delicious Deli, I felt as if I was about to spend my last six working days at the Garden of Eden. All of a sudden no one standing around in that crush was a dirty, unkempt college kid. Everyone standing or sitting was a beautiful human being. They were people with feelings and brains, and even if I never got a cent out of being there, I loved every one of them. I didn't want to have to quit working there, ever. Even when I'd be seventeen. I got a choking feeling in my chest. How could I give all this up?

I went into the back room to dump my books and wash my hands. There is a small mirror over the sink that I carefully avoided looking in. I wasn't going to let the sight of me make me feel worse.

In the kitchen, Sam was getting trays ready for me. He greeted me with, "You sure have two good lookin' brothers, Rona."

I could have done without that reminder.

"That Kenny in particular. A regular heartbreaker."

I made some kind of a sound, keeping my real feelings to myself.

"Okay, cutie," he said handing me a tray, "bring this to the take-out."

Cutie did it. I absolutely lost control and ran out of there straight to the ladies' room. After a teeming cry, I composed myself and started back. Naturally I felt embarrassed about how I'd acted. What would Sam think? I'd have to make up something even if it would be mortifying, such as that I had to go to the john urgently. When I got back in the kitchen, I noticed a small bowl of soup on the counter near the door.

"Your father made it this morning, Rona. Tell me if it's any good." Sam wasn't even looking at me.

"Thanks, Sam." I told him the soup was good. It was.

I took the trays, and I still had a rotten heavy feeling in my chest.

"What's the special special for today, Rona?"

The question came from table six. Jim, Cliff and Jerry.

The painful feeling in my chest disappeared. Another, quite different feeling took its place. I'm not sure I can describe it, but it felt very good. Like a nothing-else-matters-except-what-is-happening-right-now-feeling.

"The special special for today is . . . Wait, I'll tell you in a second." I ran over to the eat-in counter.

"Al, what's special special for today?"

"You are," he said with a slow wink.

"Oh, Al."

"Okay, our regular regulars are special specials for to-day."

"Al, this is for special special friends."

"Oh in that case, the matjes herring rollmops are like you have never!"

Al has a way of not quite finishing sentences and you're supposed to imagine the endings. I imagined he meant the herring was well worth ordering.

"Three matjes, Al, with everything."

"Three matjes with everything coming up," he practically chanted.

I took the trayful to table six.

"Al says this is like you have never," I said handing out the plates.

"Let me guess," Jerry said. He stabbed a chunk, and started chewing.

"Well?" Cliff asked.

"Think I'll try another bite."

"Hey, come on, just tell us what's in it," Jim interrupted.

"It's a filet of herring wrapped around a pickle and marinated in brine. Otherwise known as a rollmop. And by the way, Rona, you tell whoever made this that she makes rollmops almost as good as my grandmother."

"It's not a she, it's a he."

"Who is that?"

"My father."

"See, men," Jerry said, "I knew Rona came from good stock."

Jim and Cliff dug into their rollmops. As I turned to leave I noticed a girl with glasses coming toward table six. She was a little heavy and not very pretty. I figured she was a classmate of theirs. That is until she walked up to Cliff and ran her fingers right through his hair.

Boy, some nerve, I thought. He is not going to like that. From her, anyway. He looked up. Then he gave her a big, happy smile and they kissed each other right on the mouth.

"Diane, you made it, How was the exam?"

I knew I was staring, though I didn't mean to be rude. It was easy to see that Diane was very plain looking. Cliff isn't. In fact, he's almost as handsome as Paul. I suddenly felt as if I was in some other place. I couldn't take my eyes off her. She was wearing glasses! Not pretty, and glasses, and this big kiss deal! I was dumbstruck. Just as I was when I saw that Jerry was blind.

"It was a true-false. I hate them." Diane was telling them about the exam.

Then Jerry said, which I suppose was one of his funnies, "You don't look any the worse for it."

Diane was smiling to herself as if at some private joke. "I always look good, Jerry. You know that."

The way Cliff looked at her you would think she was Faye Dunaway with the limpid eyes. "I know it," he said.

Diane smiled at him, then she looked at me. "I would love a Coke."

I came back to earth. "Do you want herring too?"

"Just a Coke, thanks."

From the time I left that table until I brought her the Coke I was doing some very unusual type of thinking. And up to four o'clock that afternoon I was doing the same type of serious thinking. For some reason, maybe because I was so expert at my job now, it didn't seem to interfere.

At the end of the day after I told Daddy good-bye, I went into the john again. Of all the years I'd been in my father's store, I don't think I ever spent so much time in the john as I did that Monday. I wanted to be alone for a while because an awful lot of mixed-up ideas were in my head. Like a tossed salad.

Diane isn't beautiful, I kept thinking. She's not even pretty. And she even wears glasses. But the most surprising thing is she looks happy. Like Jerry, too, and he can't even *see*. She doesn't wear contacts either. I guess she doesn't need them. Doesn't *need* them? I need them. But *she* doesn't. Why?

I was getting pretty close to the right answer when Cathy came in, and my time was up. "Hi, Cathy. I was just leaving."

I left by the back door and walked through the parking lot behind the building. As soon as I got around the corner, the answer hit me.

It hit me hard.

Chapter 10

I ran up the three flights most likely beating my own speed record. No one was home yet. Great. I called Sharon.

"Shar, I've got to see you! Very important."

"Where were you, Rone? I came to the store at six past four and you were gone."

"That's what's very important. Meet you at Buswell in five?"

"Check."

I don't know why I said five. Ordinarily it takes us a half. I was there in a half and so was she.

"Shar," I breathed at her. "Shar, I just don't know how to tell you this."

"What, Rone, what?" She was in a tizzy of excitement, as my grandmother would say.

"I don't need contacts." I said it like the President of the United States would say, "Automobiles will be banned from the highways."

Sharon's divine golden-brown eyes almost crossed over each other.

"You don't need contacts," she repeated as if she'd been hit by one of the banned automobiles.

"Right, Shar. I don't need contacts."

We were eyeball-to-eyeball, separated only by my eyeglasses, which didn't seem ugly anymore.

"Uh . . . what . . . ."

"Shar," I said, "do you know what the most important thing in the world really is? Really?"

"You mean having a shape like mine and being cool?"

That sounded like a hundred million years ago.

"No, Shar, no. What's really important is—well, if you don't wear glasses you probably couldn't really understand," I said with a feeling of being older and more experienced than Sharon. "It's like seeing rainbows or something beautiful out of your glasses instead of . . . I mean, it's what you *make* things look like."

"You've been psyched! Where *were* you after you quit work today?"

"In my father's john."

"You were in your father's *what?*"

"In the ladies' room at Cooper's Delicatessen, to be explicit."

"That's where you got the message about the contacts?"

"Yes. Well, not exactly. You see, I was waiting on Jerry and his friends, Cliff and Jim—"

"You mean Jerry, the blind one?"

"Shar, you don't think of him as 'the blind one.' You think of him as Jerry. He's like everybody else." That was the wonder of it.

"Are his friends blind too?"

"No, Shar. In fact, Cliff has eyes that are like Paul's, almost. Anyway, there we are talking and serving and eating, and Cliff's girl friend comes in."

I stopped, picturing the two of them. The image was so clear in my mind I think Sharon was seeing it too.

"Yeah," she said encouragingly.

"Well, she looked so great—"

"Your sex-symbol type, huh?"

"No, Shar. That's the crazy thing. Practically drab . . . with glasses!"

"I get the picture."

"But you don't, Shar. After I sat there—"

"Where?"

"In the *john*, I told you!"

"Why did you pick that room?"

"It was the closest place I could be alone in. But actually, it wasn't until I was on my way home that I knew what's important about a human being. And it certainly isn't his outside beauty."

I remembered what my mother said about glasses not making a person homely or beautiful.

"It's the inside," I went on. "Like . . . like a birthday present that's wrapped up with fancy paper and ribbons. When you throw all that away, it's what's inside the box that's important."

"Well, Rona Cooper, for gosh sakes, how do you think I've been looking at you? If you were my friend for your good looks . . . . Boy, Rone. I mean real friends are friends not because of what they look like, right?"

"Right. You know what, Shar? I am your friend even though you have beautiful eyes and a terrific shape."

A certain smile that Sharon and I exchange when we know exactly what the other one means came on our faces.

Then I said, "Gee, Shar, you don't know what a load off my head this is. Now I don't have to make up stupid poems and try to sell them to earn money for contacts. Oh boy, I will never have to make up one—not even one dumb line." I was practically dancing on the sidewalk.

"Not even for the editor in chief of the Horace Mann *Horn?*" Sharon had this innocent stare.

"Not even—" Then I realized who the editor was. "I haven't thought of him all day. Oh well, Shar, for Paul Wallace I would do one or two."

"If he asked you real hard, you mean?"

"That's right. Reely, reely hard."

We enjoyed that.

"Hey, I've got to go now."

"Okay. See you in the A.M."

"Right. At the usual."

I ran or skipped or danced home. Boy, some relief. No more poems. No more worries.

Mr. Rogers' voice was singing, if you call it singing, on the T.V., which meant the boys were home and also my mother, since those kids of course don't get a key.

I went in the kitchen. "Hi, Mom. Anything I can do?"

I was feeling great until I looked at my mother. She was fumbling with stuff she was taking out of the refrigerator. When she stood up I could tell nothing had moved forward toward straightening out her marital problem. That's what it was, really—a marital problem.

She didn't speak.

"What's for dinner?" I didn't know what else to say and the silence bothered me.

She answered, "Colonel Sanders." It came out pretty throaty.

"Oh." Speaking for Daddy, I could have said, "Ugh."

I really wanted to tell her how great I felt. Maybe it would cheer her up to know one of us had cause for happiness. But since she didn't know I was planning to buy contacts in the first place, she couldn't be glad I had changed my mind in the second place.

"I'll . . . I'll set the table."

When I get married, I was thinking, I am going to settle things like this early on. He will know from the beginning that I will have a career of my own choosing and that I will not cook or . . . .

"Stop that!"

Whispering Kenny Cooper, probably kicking his brother and making it sound as if it was the other way around. I finished the sentence about planning my future. Or have boy children.

A key turned in the front door. Something dropped in the kitchen and I ran in there.

"It's only a pot," my mother explained. "Nothing in it." My father stood at the kitchen doorway. My mother was on her way up from picking the pot and when she stood as far as she was tall, they just looked at each other. Neither said a word. I got the feeling my presence wasn't needed, so I squeezed by Daddy into the dining room and busied around setting the table. In between I naturally could hear their conversation—the important parts, anyway.

After the opening remarks such as "You're home early," "So are you," they got down to basics.

"Dorothy," my father began, sounding absolutely bashed, "if it's that important to you, I understand and I—"

She cut in before he could go on. "No, Arnie, I don't think you do understand. I have found out what I really want and—"

It was his turn to cut in. "Honey, I know I haven't been fair. After all, you're entitled—"

"Arnie." My mother raised her voice now. "Arnie, I am leaving Charlotte. There is only one job I want."

There was no sound in there for quite a time, maybe seven seconds.

"Oh, honey." That was Daddy. I think the next few seconds were spent in reconciliation, like hugging and stuff.

Well, I was glad for them. After all, they're my parents and it's a lot better living around here when everyone's happy. Well, not one hundred percent everyone. There was going to be something missing in my life not working in the deli. I couldn't help feeling sad. For myself, I mean.

I heard Daddy say, "Would you make that a job and a half, Dorothy? Half time in Cooper's business has really been picking up lately and I could use extra help."

"You mean in addition to the lovely young lady?"

"What lovely young lady? One of the student customers asked me if she could work part-time. I told her if a job became available, maybe. But with you and Rona, who needs strangers?"

My heart was hammering. *Rona!* I ran in the kitchen.

"Daddy, you mean I can stay?"

"Well, I'll tell you, sweetheart. I think all things considered, until you're fourteen, would you come in just on Saturday mornings?"

"Would I? Oh, very, very neat! Then I could go to Glee Club Meetings, try out for things when they have tryouts, and, oh golly, maybe the job is still open on the editorial staff of the *Horn!* Saturday mornings—super, Daddy!"

"Only one thing," my father said solemnly.

"Wh . . . what?"

"Your bonus will have to be enlarged."

"I'll take it!"

So the way I figure it, everything worked out for the best. I mean I saved $200, which, after I earn that much from working in my father's delicatessen, I'm going to put away toward my college tuition. Those two creepy kids can earn their own way.

Just one more thing.

The next morning as I was getting ready for school, my mother called me. I figured I was going to get the word on what I was supposed to do about fixing food for dinner.

"Rona, honey, I've been thinking," she was saying it as if she was doing her thinking while she was talking. Maybe she was going to say we'd eat out tonight.

"You know, contacts aren't such a bad idea. If you still need them when you get in your teens, we might . . . ."

"Oh Mom, Mom!"